Black Voices in STEM: Reshaping the Future

By

Dominique A. Clervill

Published by Kingmaker Press, LLC 2024.

Book cover design: Dominique A. Clervill.

Artwork Illustrations: Jazziah Jones and Yancy Jones.

"You were born from a ray of God's majesty and have the blessings of a good star. Why suffer at the hands of things that don't exist? Come, return to the root of the root of your Self. You are a ruby embedded in granite."

— Rumi

Table of Contents:

Introduction

The technology industry is a vibrant and transformative force, reshaping our world in remarkable ways. From revolutionary medical innovations that save lives to tools that redefine the way we communicate and conduct business, technology's potential to improve society is boundless. Yet, amid all this progress, there's an undeniable gap - a lack of diversity that prevents the full potential of the industry from being realised.

This book is not just a call to action but a celebration. It is about encouraging a new wave of talent from underrepresented backgrounds to enter the fields of **STEM** (*Science, Technology, Engineering, and Mathematics*) and to recognise the power of code as a tool for change. By diversifying the voices and perspectives that drive technological advancements, we ensure that the systems being built work for everyone, not just a select few.

For young people of colour, particularly, representation is key. Seeing someone who looks like them succeeding in technology, can ignite a spark, opening their eyes to new possibilities and letting them know that they belong in this ever-evolving space. That is why, in this book, I have brought to light the incredible contributions of Black pioneers in technology - from trailblazing innovators to rising stars - whose stories serve as beacons of hope and inspiration. Imagine a young person realising that one of the founding members of Hewlett-Packard's computer division, responsible for developing the company's first computer, shares their background and heritage. It is moments like these that turn aspirations into realities.

As we venture into the future of technology, the importance of diversity and inclusion cannot be overstated. Together, we can dismantle the barriers that have held back so many talented individuals and build an industry that truly reflects the richness of our society. Join me in honouring the Black visionaries, who have already shaped the technological world, and in inspiring the next generation to continue breaking boundaries. Let us create a future where anyone, regardless of their background, can contribute to the world of technology - and, in doing so, change the world for the better.

Welcome to this journey of discovery and celebration. Let us give credit where it is long overdue and open the door for those who will follow.

Byron Auguste, President & Co-Founder, Opportunity@Work

The first person we will recognize is Byron Auguste who is the President & Co-Founder of Opportunity@Work. This non-profit organisation aims to expand access to quality jobs and career advancement opportunities for individuals who face roadblocks to economic success.

As a PhD economist and former White House economic policy official, Auguste understands the impact of hiring processes that only consider those with college degrees. He says that skilled workers are often overlooked, especially people from marginalised communities. Auguste notes that excluding people who don't have a bachelor's degree eliminates almost 70% of African Americans, 80% of Latino and Latina workers, and almost 80% of rural Americans of all races.

Opportunity@Work advocates for employers to recognize the overlooked talent pool of the 70 million Americans who are Skilled Through Alternative Routes (STARs). Auguste believes that hiring needs to catch up to learning and that this is the golden age of new ways to learn new skills. He explains that old, backward-looking bases for hiring need to transition to a skills-based approach.

Auguste's dedication to addressing economic inequality and creating opportunities for marginalised communities stems from his personal experience growing up in a low-income, African American family in Washington, D.C. He attended Morehouse College and later functioned as a management consultant before co-founding the non-profit organisation called Hope Street Group in 1998. Auguste has also served in the Obama Administration as a senior advisor on jobs and competitiveness and as the deputy director of the National Economic Council. His work has been widely recognized

Lisa Gelohter, CEO and Co-founder of tEQuitable

We now travel to Lisa Gelobter who is the CEO and Co-founder of tEQuitable. Lisa Gelobter is a computer scientist and technology executive who has dedicated her career to promoting diversity and inclusion in the tech industry. She is the CEO and Co-founder of tEQuitable, a platform that helps companies address and resolve workplace harassment and discrimination.

Gelobter has worked on several pioneering Internet technologies and created products that have been used by billions of people. She played a key role in the development of Shockwave, one of the first widely used animation software programs.

She also contributed to the development of **Hulu**, the streaming video platform that revolutionised the way people consume television and movies.

Gelobter's innovations have been crucial to the ascent of online video and she is widely credited with helping to create the digital media landscape as we know it today. Her contributions to internet technologies also include the animation tools necessary for the GIFs that liven up text messages and online chats.

GIF – An image file that contains multiple still or static images and plays them in order. It is a type of animation often used for humorous purposes.

Throughout her career, Gelobter has been a strong advocate for underrepresented groups in tech. She has served on the boards of several organisations focused on diversity and inclusion, including Change.org and the National Center for Women & Information Technology.

As a woman of colour in the tech industry, Gelobter has spoken publicly about the challenges she has faced and has been open about her experiences with workplace discrimination and harassment. Despite these obstacles, she remains a trailblazer in the tech world and a role model for aspiring technologists from diverse backgrounds.

Ayanna Howard, Roboticist, Entrepreneur and Educator

We have now arrived at Ayanna Howard who is a roboticist, entrepreneur and professor. She has made significant contributions to the field of robotics and artificial intelligence (AI). She is known for her work in creating robots that are able to interact with humans in a natural and intuitive way.

Howard's work has focused on creating labour-saving robots that are designed to assist people with disabilities, including children with autism. Her research has helped to advance the field of assistive robotics and has led to the development of new technologies that can help to improve the quality of life for individuals with disabilities.

Howard's work in robotics and engineering has garnered considerable attention. In 2008, her SnoMote robots were internationally recognized for their ability to study the impact of climate change in such remote areas as the Antarctic ice shelves.

https://youtu.be/WejeIgo5cRc?si=M9lnufKA1YSAEpDe

She has published more than one hundred academic papers, and she has been the recipient of several prestigious awards including the 2001 Lew Allen Award for Excellence in Research from the Jet Propulsion Laboratory, the Institute of Electrical and Electronic Engineers Early Career Award in Robotics and Automation in 2005, and the National Society of Black Engineers Janice Lampkin Educator Award in 2006.

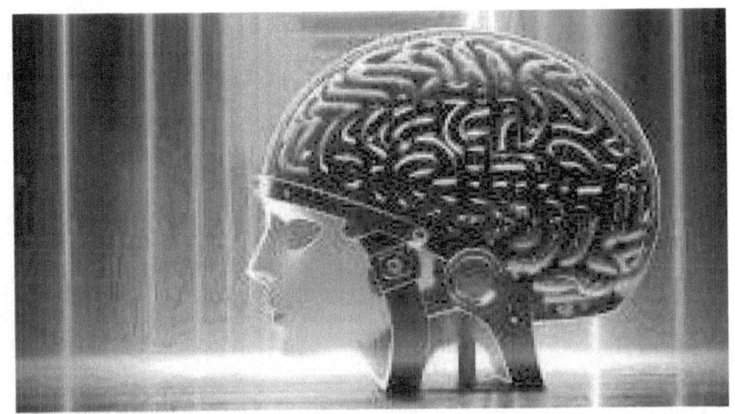

Howard has also received numerous awards for her work in robotics and AI, including the Georgia Tech Outstanding Doctoral Thesis Advisor Award and the Anita Borg Institute Women of Vision Award. She is also a Fellow of the Institute of Electrical and Electronics Engineers (IEEE).

Ayanna Howard's work in robotics and AI has had a significant impact on the field and has helped to create new technologies that can improve the lives of individuals with disabilities.

Her advocacy for diversity and inclusion in STEM has made the tech industry more equitable and inclusive, and her impact can be felt to this very day.

Clarence "Skip" Ellis, Computer Scientist

Next, we have Clarence "Skip" Ellis, a computer scientist, who was the first African American to earn a PhD in computer science, was a pioneer in the field of computer science and technology. During his time at the Palo Alto Research Center (PARC) from 1976 to 1984, Ellis headed a group that developed Officetalk, the first office system to use icons and Ethernet for remote collaboration.

His work in operational transformation, which examines functionality in collaborative systems, underpins modern remote work tools like **Google Docs**, making him a pioneer in the field of remote work. Ellis continued to work in this area, and his contributions are still found in numerous computer applications, including Apache Wave and Google Docs.

Ellis is also best known for his work in developing the first time-sharing operating system, which allowed multiple users to access a computer simultaneously. He co-founded the Association for Computing Machinery's Special Interest Group on Computer Science Education, which has been influential in promoting computer science education. In addition, Ellis was an advocate for diversity and inclusion in STEM fields, mentoring numerous students, particularly underrepresented minorities. He co-founded the Institute for African-American Mentoring in Computing Sciences, leaving behind a legacy that continues to inspire and influence generations of computer scientists and advocates for diversity in STEM fields.

Ellis received several awards and honours for his pioneering work in computer science and technology. He was named a Fellow of the Association for Computing Machinery in 1997 and received a grant from the Laboratory for New Media Strategy and Design in 2000. His contributions to the field continue to inspire generations of computer scientists and advocates for diversity in STEM fields, inspiring future generations of computer scientists. His legacy continues to impact the field today.

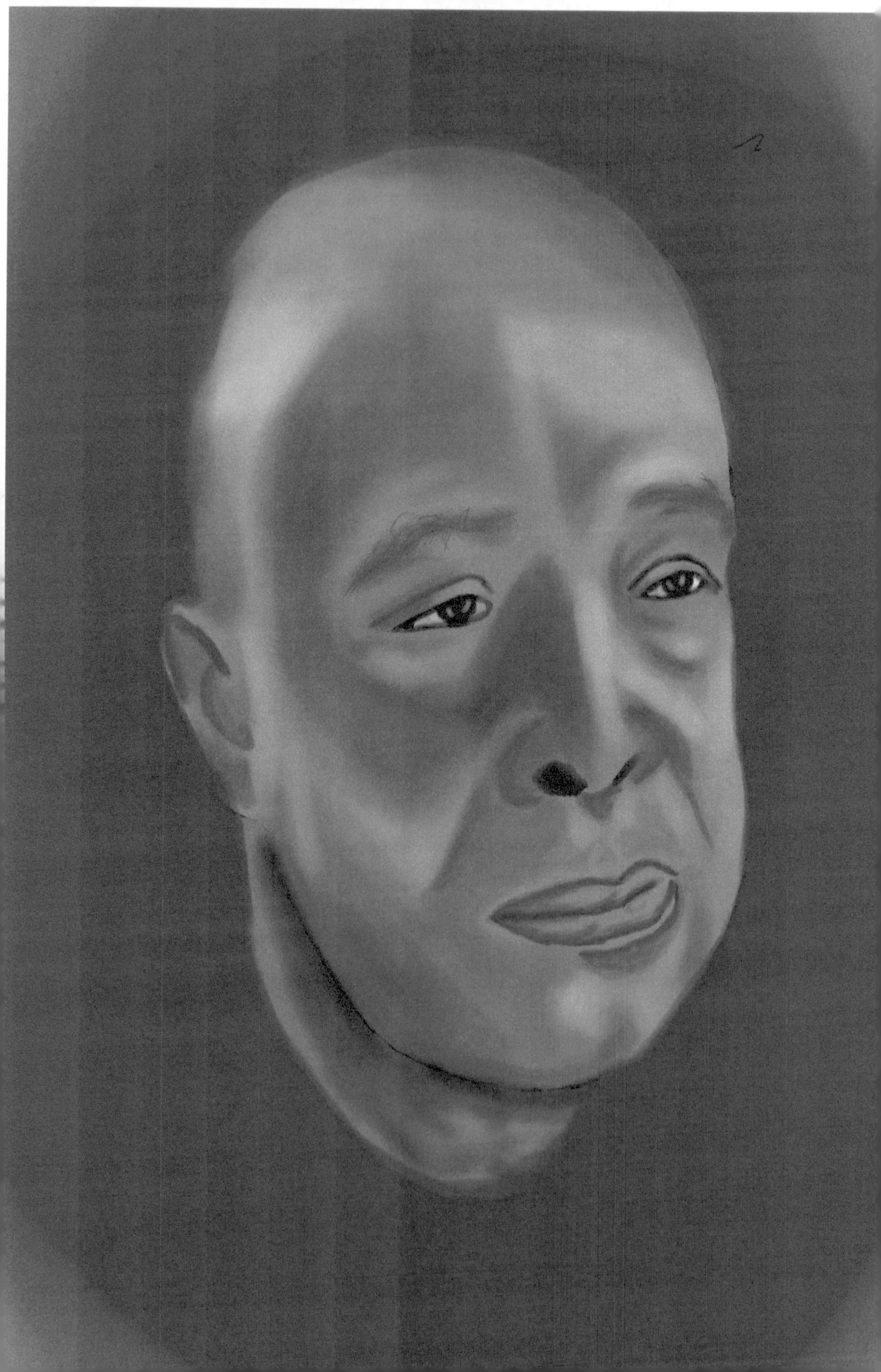

Kenneth L Coleman "Ken", Silicon Valley Executive

Now, we have Ken L. Coleman, who is a technology executive at Silicon Valley, with a long and impressive track record in the industry. He began his career in the U.S. Air Force, where he helped establish an Office for Affirmative Action and Drug Abuse Rehabilitation in 1970 at Hamilton Air Force Base.

After leaving the Air Force, he went on to work for Hewlett-Packard, where he held several senior management positions, including a two-year assignment in Northern Europe from 1974 to 1976.

Coleman's career continued to thrive, and he eventually joined Silicon Graphics (SGI) in 1987. During his fourteen years at SGI, he held several executive-level positions and managed 4,000 employees in thirty-seven countries. He was the executive vice president of sales, services, and marketing, where he made a significant impact.

In 2001, Coleman founded ITM Software in Mountain View, California. The company raised $20 million of venture capital over the next five years before being sold to BMC Software. He later served as chair of several organisations, including Accelrys, Inc., MIPS

Technologies, Saama Technologies, and EIS Group Ltd. He has also been a member of the boards of directors of several companies, including City National Bank, United Online, Entertainment Partners, Prevedere, Management Leadership for Tomorrow, CSSA Insurance, and iBridge.

Coleman's contributions to the technology industry have been widely recognized. He has received numerous honours, including The Ohio State University Distinguished Service Award and the National Alliance of Black School Educators Living Legend Award. In 1999, Coleman was named one of the ten most influential African Americans in the San Francisco Bay Area, and in 2001, one of the top 25 Black executives in technology by **Black Enterprise magazine**.

Ken Coleman is a highly respected and accomplished technology executive whose impact in the industry is hard to overstate. From his early days in the U.S. Air Force to his leadership roles at some of the industry's biggest companies, he has been a trailblazer and a role model for generations of technologists. His contributions to the industry have been significant, and his commitment to diversity and inclusion in tech has helped pave the way for a more equitable future.

Valerie Thomas, data scientist

Next, we will recognize **Valerie Thomas**, who is a data scientist and inventor known for her contributions to the development of 3D imaging and the technology that underlies modern TV and computer screens. In the 1970s, she worked for the National Aeronautics and Space Administration (NASA) and was part of a team that developed the first satellite to send images from space.

Thomas invented the illusion transmitter, a device that uses concave mirrors to create 3D images. Her technology was later used in medical imaging and television, making it possible for images to be transmitted electronically without the need for projection devices. Today, this technology is used in many industries, including medicine, aviation, and the military.

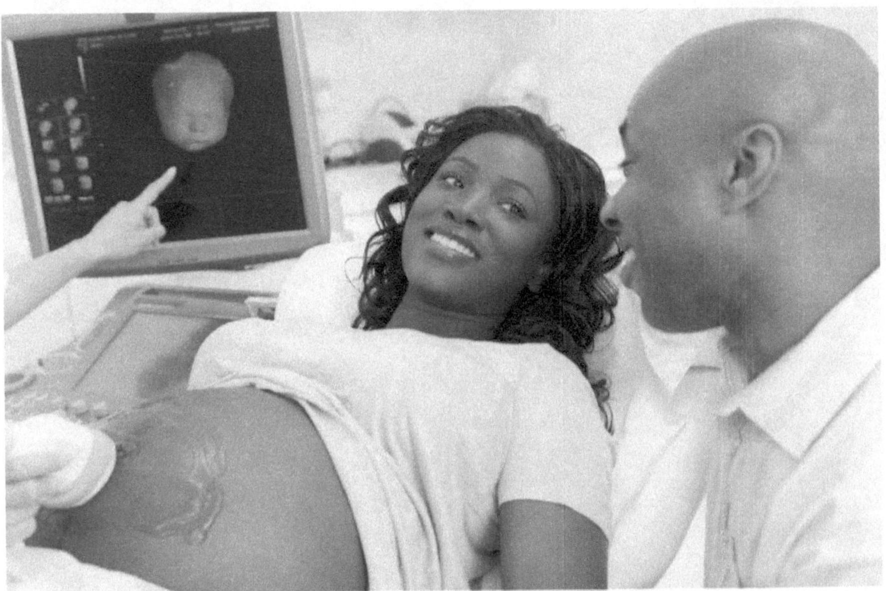

Thomas has received numerous awards for her contributions to science and technology, including induction into the National Inventors Hall of Fame. She has also been recognised for her advocacy work to encourage and inspire young people, especially girls and students of colour, to pursue careers in science and technology.

Her legacy is a testament to perseverance, hard work, and breaking down barriers to advance our understanding of the world.

Next, we will recognize Odunayo Eweniyi. She is the co-founder and Chief Operations Officer of PiggyVest, the largest digital and investment platform in Nigeria. She previously co-founded pushcv.com, one of the largest job sites in Africa with the largest database of pre-screened candidates. With 7 years of experience in Business Analysis and Operations, Eweniyi is an award-winning fintech entrepreneur who is working for diversity, equity, and inclusion in fintech and technology as a whole.

In addition to her work at PiggyVest, Eweniyi co-founded First Check Africa, a female-led angel fund that invests "ridiculously early" in women in African tech to make it easier for them to raise venture-backed capital and invest in technology startups.

She is also a board member at Village Capital, the most active supporter of impact-driven, seed-stage entrepreneurs in the world.

Eweniyi has been widely recognised for her work, including being featured on Bloomberg Business Weekly's 2020 Bloomberg50 list, an annual list of innovators, entrepreneurs, and leaders who have changed the global business landscape over the past year. She is also a 2021 TIME100 Next honoree, a Forbes Africa 30 under 30 Technology in 2019 awardee, and one of 30 Quartz Africa Innovators 2019.

As a women's rights activist, Eweniyi co-founded The Feminist Coalition, a group of young Nigerian feminists who work to promote equality. Through her work, Eweniyi aims to bring more women into entrepreneurship and advocate for the empowerment of girls and women.

Iyinolowa Aboyeji, Founder of Andela & Flutterwave

The next person we will recognize is Iyinoluwa Aboyeji. He is an entrepreneur and tech innovator who has co-founded two successful startups in Africa and is the founder and general partner of Future Africa. Aboyeji's first venture was Andela, a talent accelerator that recruits and trains software developers and connects them with employers. Andela received a $24 million investment from Mark Zuckerberg of

Facebook and has gained international recognition for its innovative approach to tech talent development.

Aboyeji's second venture, Flutterwave, is a provider of technology and infrastructure solutions for digital payments across Africa. The company has raised significant funding and has become one of Africa's most valued fintech organisations, with a valuation of $3 billion and unicorn status achieved in 2021.

Aside from his entrepreneurial ventures, Aboyeji has a strong commitment to promoting the development of the tech ecosystem in Africa. He has advised numerous national and sub-national governments across the continent on how to support high-growth innovation-driven enterprises in their domains. Aboyeji is the founder and general partner of Future Africa, a fund manager that invests early in mission-driven founders solving hard problems for large markets.

The company provides capital, coaching, and community for mission-driven innovators to build an African Future where purpose and prosperity are within everyone's reach. In addition, Aboyeji trains and mentors budding techpreneurs, equipping them with the necessary skills and knowledge to expand and take advantage of funding opportunities

Aboyeji sits on the board of several institutions, including Paris' Share Africa Project, Rainbow Educational Services Limited, and Filmo

Realty. He served as the Deputy Director-General for Madam Oby Ezekwesili's 2019 Presidential Campaign. Aboyeji is a recipient of several awards and honours, including the John C. Holland Award for Youth Leadership in 2010, Nigeria's top 20 under 20 award in 2011, World Economic Forum Global Shaper in 2012, Forbes 30 under 30 Most Promising Young Entrepreneurs in Africa in 2015, and he was nominated for The Future Awards Africa Nigeria Prize for Young Person of the Year 2017. Aboyeji's work and contributions have made him a leading figure in the African tech industry and a role model for aspiring entrepreneurs from diverse backgrounds.

Christopher Young, Executive Vice-President of Business Development at Microsoft

Next, we have Christopher Young, who is a technology industry leader and has made significant contributions to the field of business development. He is a strong advocate for technology inclusion and has worked to promote diversity and inclusion in the industry. His legacy is a testament to his leadership, innovation, and dedication to advancing the technology industry.

Christopher Young is a business development leader who has made significant contributions to the technology industry. He is currently focused on driving **Microsoft's** business development strategy in key areas such as cybersecurity, data privacy, and digital transformation. With over 25 years of experience in the industry, Young is recognised for his ability to identify and pursue new business opportunities that deliver value to customers and drive growth for the company.

Young is a passionate advocate for technology inclusion, recognising the importance of diversity and representation in driving innovation and solving complex problems. He has been instrumental in driving Microsoft's efforts to create a more inclusive and diverse workplace, supporting initiatives such as the company's AI for Accessibility program, which aims to empower people with disabilities through technology.

Prior to joining Microsoft, Young held leadership positions at companies such as Intel Security, Cisco, and RSA, where he helped to shape the direction of the cybersecurity industry. He is a respected thought leader in the technology industry, frequently speaking at conferences and sharing his insights on emerging trends and challenges facing the industry.

Christopher Young's impact on the technology industry and his commitment to driving inclusion and diversity in the workplace have earned him numerous accolades throughout his career. He is a visionary leader who continues to push the boundaries of what is possible and inspire others to do the same.

Erica Joy Baker, Chief Technology Officer for the Democratic Congressional Campaign Committee

Let's now pay our respects to Erica Joy Baker who has impacted the technological world in a massive way just as others previously mentioned. She has been an engineer in the San Francisco Bay Area for years and she is greatly known as a spokesperson and advocate for diversity and inclusion.

Erica Joy Baker first expressed interest in technology when she was a kid. Technology served as an aid in raising her all thanks to her mom. When Baker was old enough, her mom allowed her to participate in a technology camp, which influenced her decision at age 12 to make computers her career.

In 2015, Erica released a list of the salaries at Google, where she was recently employed. This instance made major headlines as it exposed the truth behind inequality in the workplace. Many workers then used this information to ask for a raise. There was disapproval in Baker's actions, but she, being a jovial lady who always keeps a smile on her face, stayed on her course towards fighting for equality in the workplace

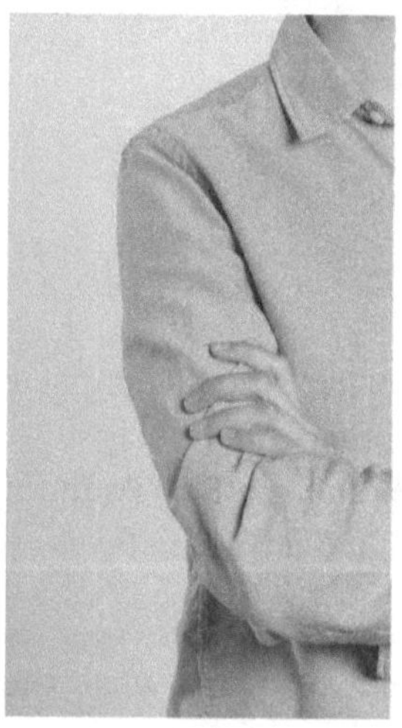
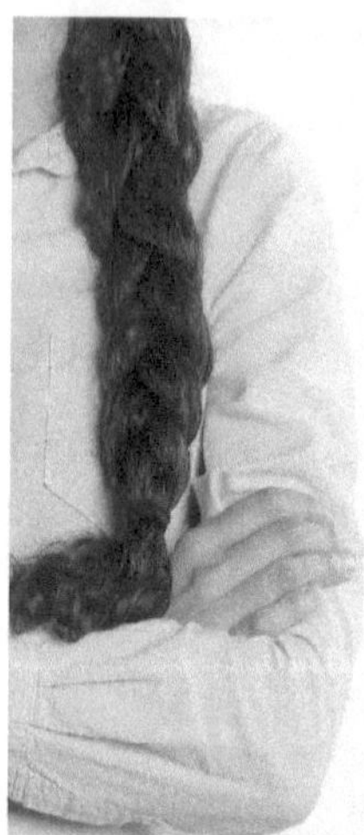

Baker remains a huge influence on the tech world by ensuring that companies show respect to all of their employees by reinforcing equality. She is a part of groups like Girls Develop It and a cofounder of the Project Include organisation, which is non-profit and uses its resources to accelerate diversity and inclusion in the workplace.

Sam Udotong, Co-founder & CTO of Fireflies.ai

Next, we have Sam Udotong, an entrepreneur and the CTO of **Fireflies.ai**, a startup that provides an AI-powered virtual assistant for note-taking during meetings. Udotong has been recognised for his entrepreneurial success and contributions to the technology industry.

After graduating from MIT with a degree in Computer Science and Aerospace Engineering, Sam Udotong turned down high-paying job offers in top tech companies to pursue his Fireflies dream. Although the initial idea of an online food delivery app did not succeed, Udotong persevered, working long hours and surviving on a meager diet to make his vision a reality. With the support of friends and his team, Fireflies has pivoted and evolved into a successful tool for transcribing video meetings into notes, raising $14 million in funding from investors who recognised its value. Fireflies.ai has built a globally-distributed team of over 100 talented individuals across 13 countries, embracing a boundaryless and asynchronous work culture while seeking exceptional engineers who share their passion for creating responsive and innovative products.

Udotong has been featured in several publications, including African Voice Online, Technext, and Business Elites Africa. He was also named in the Forbes 30 under 30 list for 2021, which recognises young entrepreneurs and leaders making significant contributions to their respective industries.

Through his work, Udotong has demonstrated the potential of African tech entrepreneurs to succeed on a global scale. He is a role model for young people who aspire to be entrepreneurs and innovators, especially those from underrepresented communities. Udotong's success is a testament to the power of hard work, determination, and a willingness to take risks to achieve one's goals.

Ime Archibong, Head of New Product Development at Facebook

Next, we have Ime Archibong, a visionary tech executive and entrepreneur who has made waves in Silicon Valley as a leader in diversity and inclusion. Currently serving as the Head of New Product Experimentation (NPE) at **Facebook**, Archibong has been recognised as one of the top Black executives in the industry, with a passion for expanding opportunities for underrepresented minorities in tech.

After earning degrees from both Yale and Stanford, Archibong began his career at IBM before transitioning to a number of other tech companies. He joined Facebook in 2010 as a product manager, where he quickly established himself as a rising star within the organisation. He went on to become the Vice President of Product Partnerships, overseeing a team responsible for integrating developers' products with Facebook's platform.

As the Head of NPE, Archibong is dedicated to exploring new product ideas and experimenting with innovative approaches to engaging users. He is an advocate for diversity and inclusion in the tech industry and has been vocal about the need for more representation of underrepresented groups. He has spoken at various events, including Slush, a leading tech conference, about the importance of building diverse teams and fostering an inclusive workplace culture.

Archibong's inspiring story has become a beacon of hope for young people, especially those from underrepresented backgrounds, who aspire to succeed in the tech industry. He is a role model, mentor, and inspiration to many, and his contributions to the field will undoubtedly continue to shape the future of technology for years to come.

Nnena Ukuku, Co-founder of Black Founders and Venture Gained Legal

Now, we have Nnena Ukuku, a legal expert, venture capitalist, and entrepreneur who has dedicated her career to supporting startups and promoting diversity and inclusion in the tech industry. She is the Co-Founder and CEO of Black Founders Startup Ventures, an organisation that equips and connects Black entrepreneurs to help their businesses thrive in technology.

Ukuku's experience in corporate law, gained from working at leading law firms in the US, and as General Counsel for venture-backed startups, gives her a unique understanding of the legal challenges facing early-stage companies. Her dedication to promoting diversity and inclusion in the tech industry has also led her to speak publicly and be involved in several initiatives focused on underrepresented groups.

Ukuku's contributions to the tech industry have been recognised, including being named to Forbes' 30 Under 30 list in Law and Policy in 2014 and being featured in several publications. Through her work with **<u>Venture Gained Legal</u>**, a law firm she founded that provides legal counsel to startups, entrepreneurs, and investors, Ukuku is helping to build a more diverse and inclusive tech industry by supporting underrepresented founders.

In addition to her legal and investment work, Ukuku is a vocal advocate for diversity and inclusion in the tech industry. She has spoken at several conferences and events on the importance of building diverse teams and creating inclusive cultures. Ukuku also serves as an advisor to startups and organisations focused on promoting diversity and inclusion.

As a vocal advocate for diversity and inclusion in the tech industry, Ukuku has spoken at several conferences and events on the importance of building diverse teams and creating inclusive cultures. Her dedication to promoting diversity and inclusion in the tech industry makes her a leader and an inspiration for underrepresented founders and entrepreneurs.

$\dfrac{d^2 G}{dr^2} + \left(\dfrac{1/4\, x^2 - 2m}{\sin^2 x c} \right.$

The accolades of Shirley Ann Jackson are vast. She is the first African-American woman to achieve a doctorate at MIT (Massachusetts Institute of Technology) in theoretical elementary particle physics, the first African-American to achieve a doctorate at MIT in any discipline and she is the second African-American woman in the United States to achieve a doctorate in physics!

Born on August 5, 1946 in Washington, D.C, she was always a person interested in STEM. After being inspired by the space race of the 1950's, she wanted to build her own projects and started studying the environment, even as young as ten years old. In high school, she took advanced math and science classes and became the valedictorian of her graduating class at Roosevelt Senior High School.

As one of only two African-American female undergraduates, the racism that she experienced motivated her to create MIT's black student union and pushed efforts to bring more potential black students to the college. Her success also led to a summer program called Project Interphase which provided assistance to minority freshmen.

Shirley Ann Jackson earned a bachelor's degree in physics *and* a Ph.D from MIT in particle physics. Her child-like curiosity in altering the world around her also led to huge contributions to inventions that we enjoy today including touch-tone telephones, caller ID, call waiting, and fiber-optic cables which greatly increased the efficiency of high-speed internet.

She would later become the head of the NRC (Nuclear Regulatory Commission) under President Bill Clinton in 1995, helping the world on an international level to promote safe and clean nuclear energy. She would eventually become the president of RPI (the Rensselaer Polytechnic Institute), becoming the first African-American woman to be the president of a major technological institute. She was later appointed a cochair of the

President's Intelligence Advisory Board and she was on Barack Obama's President's Council of Advisors on Science and Technology from 2009-2014.

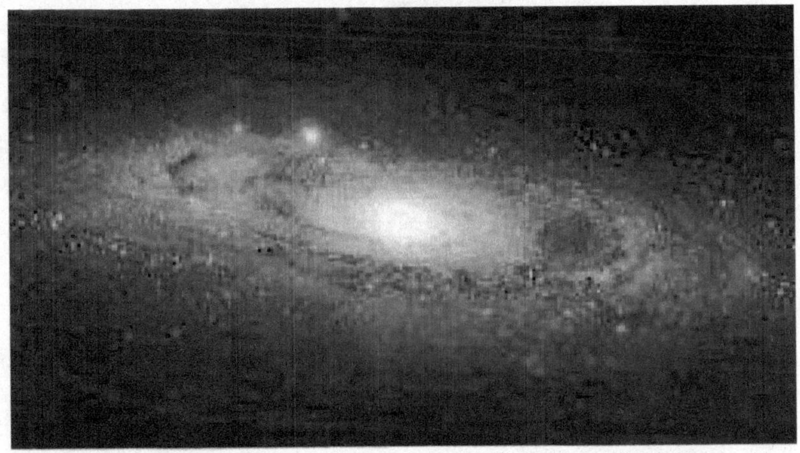

      With all of these achievements, it's no wonder that she was inducted into the National Women's Hall of Fame, was awarded the National Medal of Science by President Obama, and was given the W.E.B Du Bois Medal – a highly lauded medal given to important contributors to African American culture and society. She is a powerful and very inspirational individual and pioneer for all young black men, women and children of all ages.

looking for a dynamic and inspiring speaker who can motivate your team and energize your organization, look no further than Tony Prophet.

Dr. Erich Jarvis, the neuroscience of speech, language & music

Next, we have, Dr. Erich Jarvis who is a highly respected and accomplished neuroscientist whose groundbreaking research on the neural mechanisms of speech, language, and music has captivated both the scientific community and the general public.

As a professor of neurobiology and head of the Laboratory of Neurogenetics of Language at Rockefeller University, Jarvis has dedicated his career to investigating the molecular, cellular, and circuit-level mechanisms of vocal learning in both humans and songbirds.

With a passion for uncovering the underlying genetics and neural circuits that drive vocal learning, Jarvis's research has identified specific genes involved in this complex process and revealed striking similarities between vocal learning across species. His work is a fascinating exploration into the power and potential of the human mind, and has earned him numerous prestigious awards, including the National Institutes of Health Director's Pioneer Award and the National Science Foundation's Alan T. Waterman Award.

Beyond his groundbreaking research, Jarvis is a champion for diversity and inclusion in the sciences, actively mentoring young scientists from underrepresented groups and advocating for a more equitable and inclusive scientific community. His dedication to advancing the field of neuroscience and promoting diversity and inclusion is an inspiration to all, and his work serves as a powerful reminder of the incredible potential of the human mind.

Whether you are a scientist, student, or simply curious about the wonders of the brain, Dr. Erich Jarvis's work is sure to leave you inspired and fascinated.

Mary Jackson, Mathematician and Aerospace Engineer

Born on April 9, 1921, Mary Jackson was a testament to the resilience of the human spirit. She was born in Hampton, Virginia—a place with a tumultuous history. It is known for receiving the first African slaves in America in 1619, as well as a major revolt in 1861 in which enslaved men and women fought back for their freedom, marking one of the first events leading to slavery's collapse. Less than a hundred years later, Mary Jackson would lead the charge towards excellence.

After graduating from high school with the highest honor, she would go on to receive two degrees in mathematics and physical science at what is now known as Hampton University in 1942. In 1951, she worked for NACA, the National Advisory Committee for Aeronautics (which would later merge into NASA), working on equations vital to the U.S space program. Despite her achievements, the program was still very much segregated, meaning that she still had to eat in separate places from her white counterparts. Still, her accomplishments gained the attention of her boss, who encouraged her to become an engineer.

In 1958, despite a school that was also segregated, she became the first Black female engineer in NASA.

Working hard for the next 20 years, she fought for women's rights in the workplace, even taking a demotion from her role to become the manager of the women's program at NASA in 1979. Her incredible work has been recognized for her contributions to NASA and its future. One notable highlight was that she inspired one of the main characters in Margot Lee Shetterly's book, Hidden Figures: The American Dream and the Untold Story of the Black Women Mathematicians Who Helped Win the Space Race. A movie was made based on the book in 2016, inspiring millions of young girls to reach for the stars!

Roy Clay Sr., Computer Scientist

Next, we have Roy Clay's remarkable journey as a pioneering engineer, entrepreneur, and public servant that has left an indelible mark on the technology sector, inspiring countless individuals to chase their dreams. As an influential computer engineer and programmer, Clay played a critical role in shaping the early days of Silicon Valley and laid the foundation for its future growth.

Having started his career at Control Data Corporation as one of the first programmers, Clay's talent was undeniable. His expertise caught the attention of **Hewlett-Packard**, who brought him on board in 1965 to establish and lead their computer division. Under Clay's guidance, HP's computer division flourished, and he was instrumental in the development of the groundbreaking HP 2116A minicomputer. This accomplishment not only solidified HP's status as a technology powerhouse but also cemented Clay's reputation as an innovative force.

Roy Clay's entrepreneurial spirit led him to establish ROD-L Electronics in 1977. The company specialized in manufacturing electrical safety testing equipment and swiftly rose to prominence as an industry leader. With numerous accolades to its name, ROD-L Electronics remains synonymous with reliability and high-quality products.

In addition to his professional accomplishments, Roy Clay has also made significant contributions to his community. He was elected Vice Mayor of Palo Alto in 1976, showcasing his dedication to public service. Clay has served on various boards and committees, such as the Palo Alto History Museum and the Palo Alto Community Fund. As a founding member of the Silicon Valley Black Chamber of Commerce, Clay has been instrumental in promoting African American entrepreneurship and economic growth in the region.

Roy Clay's incredible story of perseverance, innovation, and dedication to fostering diversity, opportunity, and community engagement serves as a powerful reminder that with hard work and determination, anything is possible. His groundbreaking work in technology, visionary leadership at HP, entrepreneurial success with ROD-L Electronics, and commitment to public service have not only earned him a place in history as a true Silicon Valley pioneer but also made him a role model for generations to come.

Erica Jefferson, President and Founder of Black Women in Science and Engineering (BWISE)

Next, we have Erika Jefferson, a distinguished chemical engineer and passionate advocate for diversity in science, technology, engineering, and mathematics (STEM). She is the inspiring Founder and President of Black Women in Science and Engineering (BWISE). BWISE is a non-profit organization dedicated to elevating the voices, achievements, and opportunities for Black women in STEM, addressing the persistent underrepresentation and lack of visibility for this dynamic group of professionals.

Fueled by her personal experiences and a deep understanding of the unique challenges faced by Black women in STEM, Jefferson established BWISE to create an empowering and supportive community. Through mentorship programs, networking events, professional development workshops, and collaborative partnerships with industry leaders, BWISE fosters an inclusive environment where Black women can flourish and excel in their respective fields.

Jefferson's educational background includes a dual BS in Chemical Engineering degree from Louisiana Tech University and Southern University and A&M College at Baton Rouge, as well as an MBA from Georgia Institute of Technology. Throughout her multifaceted career, she has held various roles, including process engineer, project manager, and business development manager, which have further reinforced her commitment to promoting diversity and inclusion in STEM.

An active member of the American Institute of Chemical Engineers (AIChE), Jefferson has contributed significantly to the conversation around representation in STEM. She authored an article for the Scientific American Blog Network titled "Where Are the Black Women in STEM Leadership?" Her insights and dedication have inspired countless individuals and fostered constructive dialogue on the importance of representation in STEM.

Erika Jefferson's unwavering pursuit of a more inclusive and diverse STEM landscape has resonated with countless professionals and industry leaders. Through her visionary leadership at Black Women in Science and Engineering (BWISE), she has created a vibrant community that celebrates, empowers, and advances the careers of Black women in STEM. As a result, her work continues to leave a lasting and transformative impact on the STEM workforce, inspiring future generations of Black women to pursue their dreams and overcome barriers.

Saron Yitbarek, Founder of Code Newbie and CodeLand Conference

Next, we have Saron Yitbarek, a dynamic entrepreneur, developer, speaker, and podcaster who founded Code Newbie, now owned by DEV. As the driving force behind the CodeLand Conference, she is dedicated to promoting inclusivity and diversity in the tech industry. Her work focuses on empowering underrepresented communities to succeed in the world of programming, breaking down barriers that have traditionally limited their access.

Yitbarek's transformative journey into technology began during her college years when she pursued a pre-med, double degree in psychology and English, intending to become a doctor. However, after shadowing a cardiologist, she discovered her true passion for problem-solving, rather than directly saving lives.

Taking a bold leap of faith, Yitbarek immersed herself in coding for 30 days, spending 12 to 14 hours a day mastering the craft. Despite the challenges, she found herself eager to continue learning. Her perseverance paid off as she attended a coding bootcamp and launched her career as a software developer upon graduation.

Acknowledging the critical role of a supportive community for coding learners, Yitbarek founded Code Newbie as a podcast in 2014 to share inspiring stories and experiences of people in tech. The platform has since blossomed into a thriving online community, providing resources, support, and mentorship for coding learners while hosting weekly Twitter chats and virtual events. This nurturing environment has been crucial to the success of countless individuals seeking to learn and grow in the world of programming.

Besides her work with Code Newbie, Yitbarek is an influential tech educator and public speaker, delivering keynotes at tech conferences and events worldwide. Her insights and expertise on coding, tech education, and diversity in the industry have been featured in various interviews. In 2020 , Code Newbie reached a significant milestone when it was acquired by open-source firm Forem. This acquisition allowed Yitbarek's vision to touch even more lives, as the partnership further bolstered the community and expanded opportunities for individuals from diverse backgrounds to learn and grow in the world of programming. Saron Yitbarek's unwavering dedication to breaking down barriers in the tech industry and fostering a supportive, inclusive environment for coding learners has made a profound impact on countless individuals, helping them unlock their potential and thrive in their careers.

Hadiyah Mujhid, CEO and Founder of HBCUvc

Next, we have Hadiyah Mujhid who is a pioneering force and an advocate for diversity and equality in the tech world. As the CEO and Founder of HBCUvc an organisation that provides training, education, and funding to students from historically black colleges and universities who are interested in pursuing careers in venture capital. She is relentless in her mission to provide opportunities for Black and Latinx VCs and entrepreneurs who have been previously neglected. With her wealth of experience as a tech founder and her unwavering dedication to social justice, Mujhid has established herself as a change-maker and a driving force for progress.

Mujhid's background in software engineering has equipped her with the skills necessary to excel in the rapidly evolving tech industry. However, her passion for empowering underrepresented communities stems from her own experiences as a black woman in technology. She recognizes the challenges faced by Black and Latinx entrepreneurs and VCs in securing funding and building successful businesses, and is committed to addressing this imbalance.

Through her collaborations with AnnenbergTech and PledgeLA, Mujhid is working tirelessly to promote equality for Black and Latino entrepreneurs and VCs. Her innovative approach to investing has been widely recognised, with Forbes and TechCrunch lauding her achievements.

Mujhid's leadership and unwavering dedication to social justice have inspired many to follow in her footsteps and work towards a more equitable future. Her impact on the lives of underrepresented communities in the tech and venture capital spaces is profound and long-lasting. With her unwavering spirit and commitment to creating a fairer and more inclusive world, Hadiyah Mujhid is a true innovator and a source of inspiration to us all.

NASA

Aisha Bowe, Co-Founder and CEO, Stemboard

Next, we have Aisha Bowe who is a passionate advocate for diversity and inclusion in the world of science and technology. She has played an active role in supporting women leaders in STEM through her work with various organisations such as General Assembly and the Women of Colour Engineers Council (WCEC). Her dedication to fostering a more diverse and inclusive STEM environment has made a significant impact on the lives of aspiring engineers and scientists.

Bowe's exceptional career and steadfast determination have earned her recognition. She has been selected as a future Blue Origin astronaut, further solidifying her status as a role model for young women in STEM. Additionally, she was named Entrepreneur of the Year by the Black Data Processing Associates (BDPA) of Washington, D.C., showcasing her dedication and accomplishments in the industry. She was also honoured with NASA's Engineering Honour Award.

As the CEO of **STEMBoard**, Bowe has focused on providing high-quality, cost-efficient solutions in engineering and development, IT services, program and project management, data management, and analytics. Her company's services have been instrumental in supporting clients, including government agencies and private companies, in achieving their goals and maintaining a competitive edge in their respective industries.

Bowe's dedication, talent, and perseverance make her a true icon in the realms of science, technology, and aerospace. Her exceptional career serves as an inspiration to young people, particularly women and minorities, encouraging them to pursue careers in STEM fields. As Bowe continues to break barriers and reach new heights, she is paving the way for future generations to make their mark in science and technology. Her advocacy for diversity and inclusion is helping to create a more equitable and innovative world, where the next generation of engineers and scientists can thrive and push the boundaries of what is possible.

Phaedra Ellis-Lamkins, Co-Founder and CEO of Promise, Board Member Tipping Point Community

Next, we have Phaedra Ellis-Lamkins who is a social justice advocate and businesswoman. She is renowned for her impressive work in various sectors, including technology, entertainment, and social justice. As the founder and CEO of Promise, a payment technology platform that simplifies government debt, she has utilised her expertise to benefit millions of Americans. Prior to founding Promise, Phaedra played a crucial role at Honor, a home care technology company, where she ran revenue and operations. Her impressive resume also includes working closely with the legendary musician Prince and leading the effort to secure ownership of his master recordings.

Throughout her career, Phaedra has remained committed to making a measurable change in society. In her earlier years, she served as the Executive Officer of the South Bay AFL-CIO Labor Council, representing over 100 unions and more than 110,000 members in California. Additionally, she was the Executive Director of Working Partnerships USA, a coalition of community groups, labour, and faith organisations addressing economic disparities in California's Silicon Valley. Phaedra also served as CEO of the anti-poverty organisation Green For All.

Phaedra's incredible leadership has garnered recognition from numerous esteemed platforms. The World Economic Forum honoured her as a Young Global Leader, while Essence named her one of the 25 Most Influential African Americans. She has also been featured on Ebony's Power 150, The Grio's 100 History Makers in the Making, and Black Enterprise's 40 Next: Emerging Leaders for Our Future. San Jose Magazine acknowledged her as one of the 100 most powerful people in Silicon Valley. In addition to her accomplishments, Phaedra serves on the boards of Honor and Tipping Point.

Just as Creola Katherine Coleman, widely known as Katherine Johnson, defied the odds and broke barriers in the world of mathematics and space exploration, Phaedra Ellis-Lamkins continues to champion social justice and innovation in the realms of technology and business. Her unwavering dedication and passion for creating a better world have made her an inspiring figure and a true leader in her field.

Iheanvi Ekechukwu, Software Engineer

Now, we have Iheanyi Ekechukwu, a highly accomplished software engineer who has made a name for himself in the technology industry. He has had an illustrious career working for top tech companies, such as **GitHub** and PlanetScale, and is renowned for his expertise in designing and writing code. Iheanyi is also known for his work in promoting diversity and inclusion within the tech industry, striving to share the stories and experiences of people of colour in the field.

After graduating from the University of Notre Dame with a degree in Computer Science and Engineering, Iheanyi quickly gained recognition in the industry. He went on to work as a senior software engineer at GitHub, where he focused on improving developer workflows and user experiences. His notable work there included enhancements to the platform's code review process and the development of GitHub's interactive web development tools. He then moved to PlanetScale, where he continues to hold a position as a Senior Software Engineer, further developing his expertise in software engineering and database technology.

In addition to his technical achievements, Iheanyi has a passion for sharing his knowledge with others. He has participated in numerous talks and interviews, providing insights into his work and discussing the application of design principles to the field of coding. This commitment to education extends to his advocacy for diversity within the technology sector, contributing to the publication Model View Culture and being featured by People of Colour in Tech (POCIT), where he shares his thoughts on representation and inclusion in the industry.

Iheanyi Ekechukwu is an inspiring figure in the world of software engineering, having achieved great success across various roles within the industry. Beyond his technical prowess, his dedication to promoting diversity and inclusion within the tech sector, along with his passion for sharing knowledge, have made him an influential figure in the industry. With a career that spans numerous years and impressive achievements, Iheanyi Ekechukwu's work continues to inspire and motivate aspiring software engineers and underrepresented groups alike.

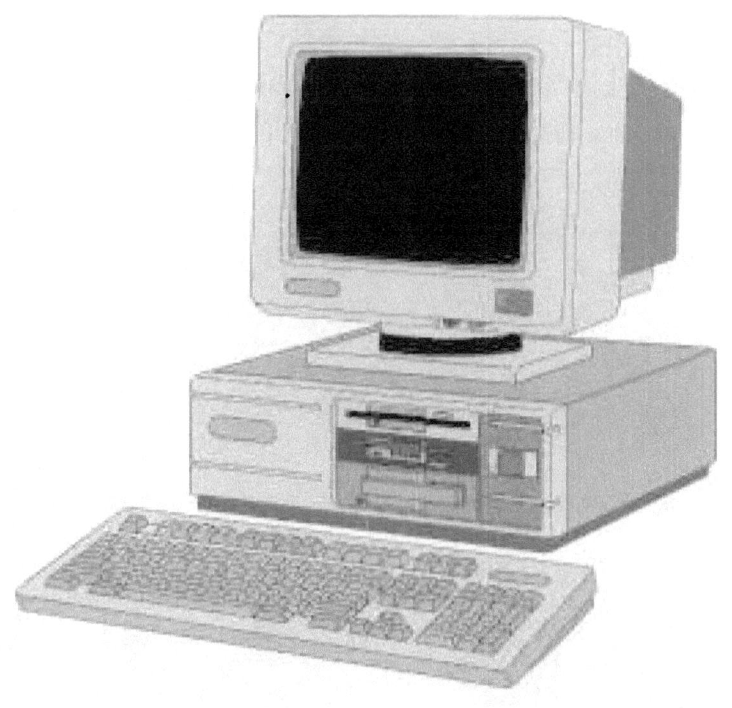

As he continues to make strides in his career, there is no doubt that there is much more to come for him. Keep an eye on Iheanyi Ekechukwu, as his pace and trajectory promise an even brighter future in the realm of technology.

Next, we have Nicholas CM Fuller. He is a distinguished technologist, IBM Master Inventor, and Vice President of Distributed Cloud at IBM Research. With over 75 patents and co-authorship of 75 technical publications, Fuller has made significant contributions to the field of computer science, artificial intelligence, and cloud computing. His research has focused on developing a comprehensive AI and platform-based edge research strategy, anchored by enterprise use cases and partnerships.

Fuller's groundbreaking work at IBM Research has led to the development of various technologies that have transformed the industry. As part of his role, he manages the Distributed Cloud Labs and oversees

IBM's comprehensive edge research strategy. His vision and leadership have resulted in numerous technological innovations, spanning from AI to cloud infrastructure. In particular, his work in distributed computing and edge technologies has led to significant advancements in real-time data processing, which enables businesses to make better-informed decisions.

In addition to his work at IBM Research, Fuller is dedicated to sharing his knowledge with the wider community. He has been featured on the Caribbean Data Science Podcast, where he discussed the impact of AI and cloud computing on modern society. Through this platform, he has engaged with experts in the field, stimulating thought-provoking discussions and sharing his expertise on distributed cloud technologies.

Fuller's contributions to the field of computer science have been widely recognized. As an IBM Master Inventor, he has been instrumental in shaping the future of technology, and his extensive patent portfolio speaks to his dedication and ingenuity. His work continues to inspire the next generation of technologists and innovators, as he remains at the forefront of his field, driving cutting-edge research and development.

Nicholas CM Fuller is an accomplished technologist and IBM Master Inventor, making lasting contributions to computer science, AI, and cloud computing. As Vice President of Distributed Cloud at IBM Research, he has played a pivotal role in shaping the future of technology through his extensive research and innovative developments. Fuller continues to inspire the next generation of technologists and remains a driving force in the advancement of the industry.

NASA

Guion "Guy" Bluford, Jr., Astronaut

Next, we have Guion "Guy" Bluford, Jr., a trailblazing astronaut who made history as the first African American to journey into space. His groundbreaking spaceflight took place on August 30, 1983, aboard the Space Shuttle Challenger STS-8 mission. Bluford's accomplishments in space exploration paved the way for future generations of diverse astronauts and continue to inspire countless individuals worldwide.

Bluford's illustrious career began with his service in the United States Air Force, where he became a decorated fighter pilot and eventually achieved the rank of Colonel. With a strong educational background, he earned a Bachelor of Science degree in aerospace engineering, a Master of Science degree in aerospace engineering, a Master of Business Administration, and a Doctor of Philosophy in aerospace engineering.

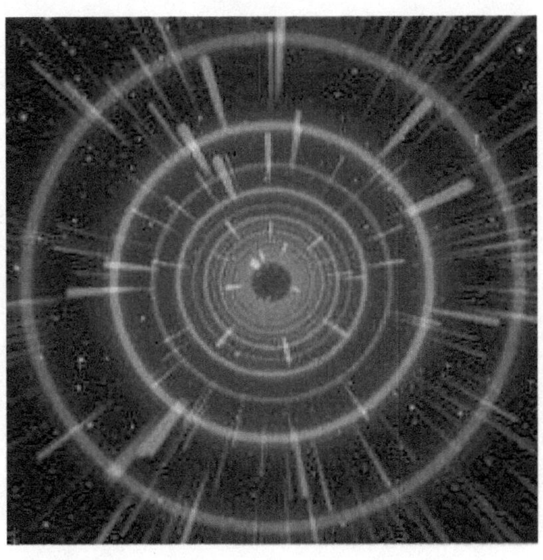

NASA selected Bluford as an astronaut candidate in 1978, and he completed his training in 1979. As a mission specialist, he took part in four Space Shuttle missions, totalling over 688 hours in space. In addition to his groundbreaking STS-8 mission, Bluford served on STS-61A in 1985, STS-39 in 1991, and STS-53 in 1992. His work during these missions included deploying satellites, conducting scientific research, and testing new technologies for space exploration.

Following his successful career as an astronaut, Bluford transitioned into the private sector. He held various executive positions at Northrop Grumman Corporation and the Aerospace Technology Group, contributing his expertise in aerospace engineering and space exploration. Bluford's outstanding work in both the public and private sectors has earned him numerous accolades, including the NASA Distinguished Service Medal, the United States Air Force Meritorious Service Medal, and the National Society of Black Engineers' Distinguished National Scientist Award.

Guion "Guy" Bluford, Jr. is a pioneering astronaut who became the first African American to venture into space, inspiring generations of diverse individuals to pursue careers in space exploration. With an exceptional educational and military background, Bluford completed four Space Shuttle missions and made significant contributions to scientific research and technology development in space. His work in both the public and private sectors, along with his commitment to breaking barriers, has left a lasting legacy that continues to inspire and shape the future of space exploration.

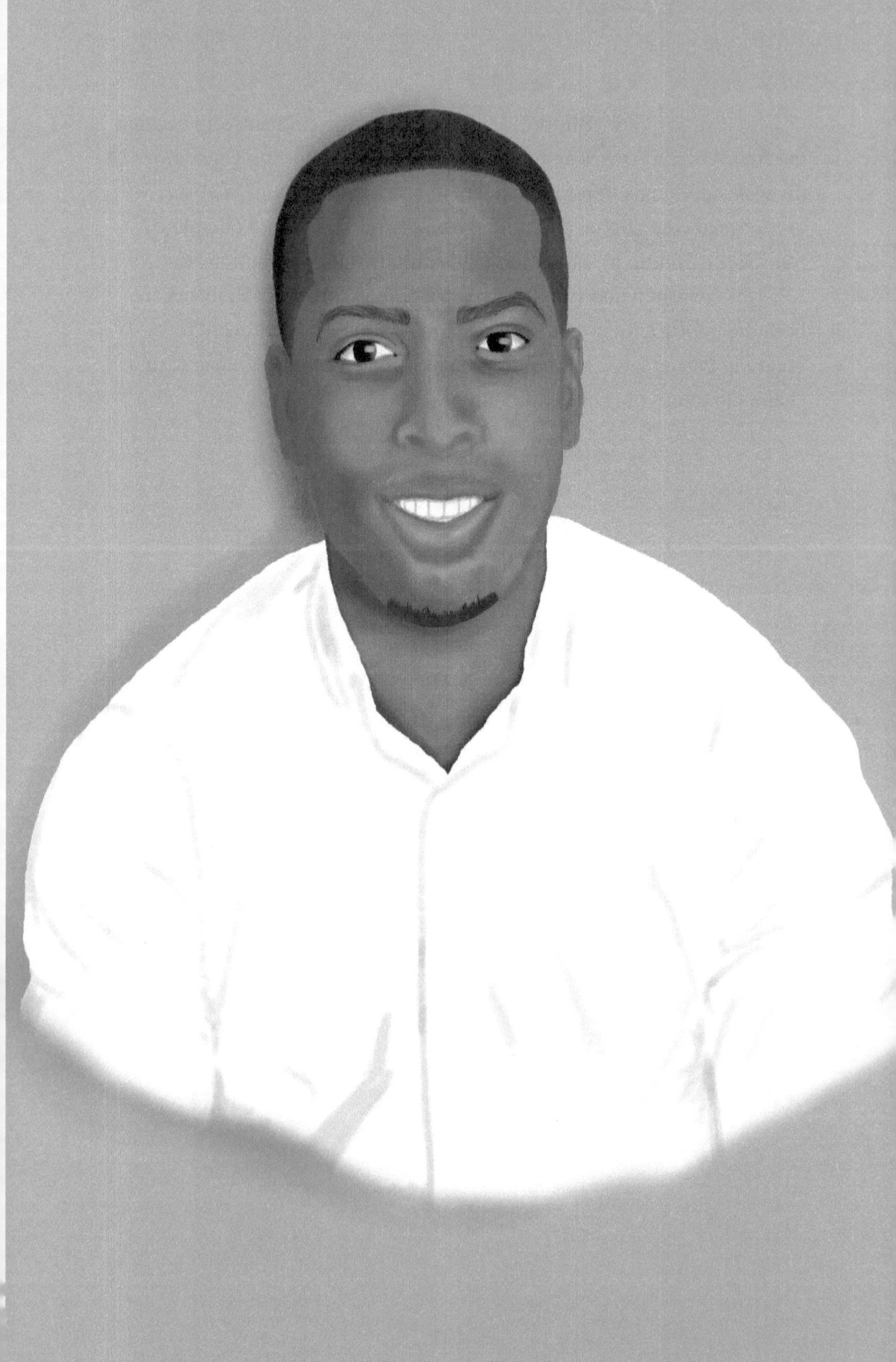

Tristan Walker, Entrepreneur and CEO of Walker & Company

Next, we have Tristan Walker who has been proven to be resilient, innovative, and triumphant. Despite facing significant adversity in his childhood in Queens, New York, Walker remained steadfast in his determination to succeed, and he has become one of the most influential entrepreneurs and investors in the tech industry.

After graduating from Stony Brook University, Walker gained invaluable experience at top-tier companies such as Foursquare and Twitter. However, it was his tenure at Andreessen Horowitz that sparked his passion for entrepreneurship. In 2013, he founded his own start-up, Walker & Company Brands, which focused on creating personal care products for people of colour. The company's success attracted the attention of Procter & Gamble, which acquired it in 2018.

Under Walker's leadership, Walker & Company Brands became a household name, with products such as Bevel and Form reaching millions of customers worldwide.

He has also been a vocal advocate for diversity and inclusion in the tech industry, serving on the boards of several non-profit organisations and founding the CODE2040 Fellowship Program to provide opportunities for underrepresented minorities in tech.

Today, Walker is a highly sought-after investor and advisor in the tech industry, with a particular focus on companies that are making a positive impact in the world. He continues to inspire others with his story of perseverance and innovation, and his unwavering commitment to creating a more inclusive and equitable tech industry.

Tristan Walker is a true trailblazer whose achievements have earned him a place among the most successful entrepreneurs of his generation. His unwavering dedication to diversity, innovation, and excellence serves as an inspiration to all those who aspire to make a meaningful difference in the world.

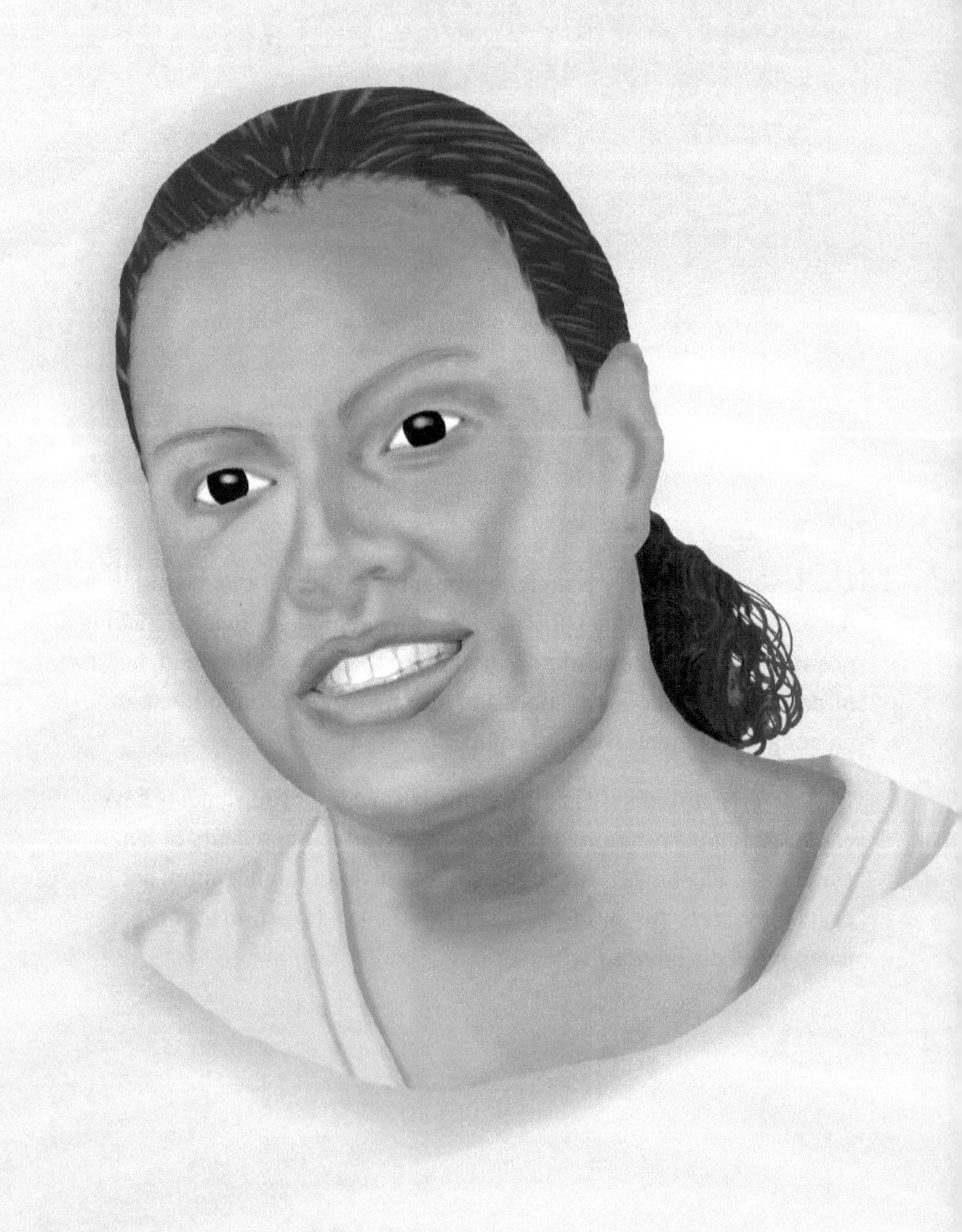

Heather Hiles, technologist and entrepreneur

Next, we have Heather Hiles, a visionary leader in the edtech and entrepreneurial spheres, who has made significant strides in transforming the landscape of education and business. Harnessing her expertise in development studies, ethnic studies, and business management, Hiles has been instrumental in creating meaningful change throughout her illustrious career.

As the CEO and Founder of Pathbrite, Hiles developed a digital portfolio platform embraced by colleges and universities. Under her leadership, the company flourished until its acquisition by Cengage Learning in November 2015. Prior to this, Hiles demonstrated her passion for empowering marginalised communities by founding SFWorks, a non-profit that trained and placed people on welfare into living-wage jobs, where she served as CEO from 1997 to 2001.

In the realm of philanthropy, Hiles worked as the Deputy Director of Postsecondary Success Solutions at the Bill & Melinda Gates Foundation from October 2016 to November 2017, focusing on combating poverty, disease, and inequity around the world. Additionally, Hiles served as the founding Chancellor and Chief Executive Officer of Calbright College, an online community college geared towards preparing students for technology industry jobs, from January 2019 to March 2020.

In August 2020, Hiles became a member of Udemy's board of directors, and currently serves as the managing partner of **Black Ops Ventures**, a seed-stage venture firm funding Black founders. Moreover, Hiles is actively involved with the boards of directors for several private companies, including the groundbreaking **Black Girls Code**.

With a remarkable track record of achievements, Heather Hiles has distinguished herself as a force for change in education and entrepreneurship, continuously pushing for innovative solutions and empowering those who are often overlooked. Her sincere dedication to fostering opportunities and creating a more inclusive landscape has made her an inspirational figure to many.

Eghosa Omoigui, Founder and Managing General Partner of EchoVC Partners

Next, we have Eghosa Omoigui, a distinguished figure in the world of venture capitalism and technology. He is the founder and Managing General Partner of EchoVC Partners. With an unwavering focus on underrepresented founders and underserved emerging markets, Omoigui has carved out a niche for himself as a visionary, connecting Sub-Saharan Africa and North America in innovative ways.

Before his success with EchoVC, Omoigui navigated the challenging yet rewarding journey at Intel Capital as the Director of Consumer Internet and Semantic Technology Engineering. His strategic investments significantly influenced Intel's consumer investment portfolio, and his expertise extended to various companies including AdMob, Jaiku, Powerset, Facebook, LinkedIn, Teracent, Qik, and Pandora.

Not just content with industry success, Omoigui has been an inspiring presence at esteemed technology and investment conferences worldwide, such as the Global Investment Summit and Africa Tech Summit Connects. Through these engagements, he actively listens and learns from others, remaining at the forefront of the ever-evolving tech industry.

Omoigui's passion for innovation is evident in his bold step with EchoVC, launching a blockchain fund focused on Africa. This commitment demonstrates his belief in Africa's technological potential and its ability to revolutionise the global tech scene.

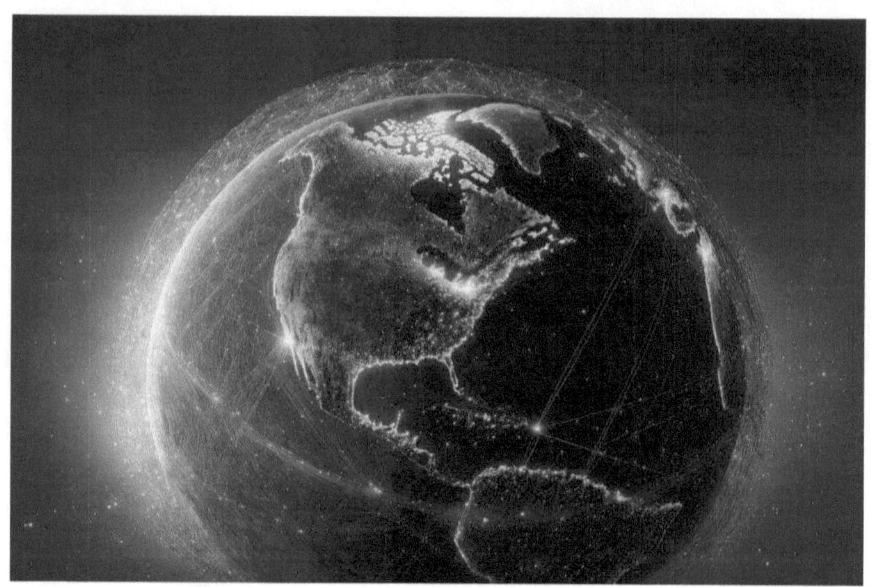

His involvement with the Global Private Capital Association (GPCA) further underscores his commitment to fostering a globally connected investment landscape. Omoigui also advises SWIFT (the inter-bank consortium) on technology innovation for financial services (InnoTribe), is a member of the ASTIA Venture Advisory Board (an organisation focused on mentoring and supporting women entrepreneurs), and is a Kauffman Fellowship and Pipeline Angel Fellowship Mentor.

Eghosa Omoigui's story is one of determination, vision, and an unwavering commitment to fostering global technological advancement. His journey from Intel to EchoVC, his influential presence at key global conferences, and his dedication to innovative technologies like blockchain paint a picture of a man who is as passionate about technology as he is about creating meaningful connections. He serves as an inspiring beacon for aspiring tech entrepreneurs and investors, proving that with vision and tenacity, one can indeed make a significant impact on the world.

Fern Hunt, Mathematician

Next, we have Fern Y. Hunt, an exceptional mathematician, who is celebrated for her profound contributions to applied mathematics and mathematical biology. She made her mark in the field during her tenure at the National Institute of Standards and Technology (NIST) where she developed innovative methods in stochastic analysis, a branch of mathematics that operates with random phenomena. Her work in this area has been instrumental in understanding and predicting complex systems, with wide-ranging implications for various scientific fields.

Her passion for mathematics and the sciences was not confined to her own research. She played an integral role in the Mathematical Association of America, where she worked diligently to bolster mathematical education and inspire the next generation of mathematicians. Her efforts in this area have been instrumental in promoting mathematics to a broad audience, showcasing its relevance and applicability in numerous aspects of everyday life.

Hunt's outstanding research led to her receiving the esteemed Arthur S. Flemming Award, underlining her remarkable contributions to the field of mathematics. This honour is testament to her expertise, pioneering spirit and dedication to her profession.

Hunt has been a champion for diversity within the scientific community. As a leading Mathematician of the African Diaspora, she has consistently advocated for the representation and inclusion of minorities in STEM fields. Her commitment to this cause has not only broken down barriers within her profession but has also paved the way for future generations of mathematicians from diverse backgrounds.

Fern Y. Hunt's career has been characterised by exceptional academic achievements, a dedication to promoting mathematics education, and a tireless commitment to diversity within her field. Her innovative research in stochastic analysis has greatly advanced our understanding of complex systems, while her efforts to promote mathematics and diversity have left a lasting legacy. Indeed, Hunt's work continues to inspire future mathematicians, particularly those from underrepresented backgrounds, setting the stage for the continued evolution of the field.

We now have Ulysses J. Smith, a guiding light within the tech industry, who embodies the spirit of change as an important Diversity, Equity, and Inclusion (DEI) Strategist. His relentless advocacy for underrepresented communities and his proven expertise have a profound, transformative impact on the landscapes he navigates, shaping a more equitable future for all.

His work as the Head of Diversity, Inclusion & Belonging at Blend, a leading fintech company based in San Francisco, stands testament to his commitment to fostering cultures of respect and inclusivity. Blend, known for its innovative digital lending platform, benefits tremendously from Smith's DEI leadership. His efforts create an internal environment defined by diversity and respect, which in turn influences the way Blend interacts with its diverse customers and the broader community.

In addition to his work at Blend, Smith carries his DEI expertise to a broad range of organisations through his private firm, Archetype. He has collaborated with companies across New York State and the San Francisco Bay Area, including Airbnb, Gusto, Genentech, and Electronic Arts. In these consulting engagements, Smith provides guidance and strategies to build more inclusive workplaces, influencing these organisations from within and making a lasting impact on their corporate culture.

Beyond these roles, Smith serves as an influential voice in broader circles. He shares his insights and knowledge on DEI strategies globally through his platform at Udemy. As part of the Human Capital Institute, he offers critical perspectives on inclusive human resource practices. Smith also champions equitable investment practices within the tech ecosystem through his role at EchoVC Partners.

Furthermore, Smith is recognised for his contributions to the Equitable Ecosystem Initiative, where he advocates for systemic change within the tech industry. This initiative amplifies Smith's vision for a tech ecosystem that embraces equity in all its aspects.

In essence, Ulysses J. Smith is not just a revered figure in the tech industry, but also a tireless champion for diversity, equity, and inclusion. His legacy of promoting systemic change and driving transformative inclusivity inspires future generations and demonstrates the profound potential of embracing diversity. Smith's story resonates with a powerful message: the commitment of one individual to inclusivity can indeed reshape an industry, inspiring us all to strive for a more equitable world.

Next, we have Tope Awotona who is a highly successful entrepreneur, renowned for founding Calendly, a leading scheduling application. With roots tracing back to Nigeria, Awotona's journey is a testament to the power of perseverance, risk-taking, and a relentless drive for success.

Awotona's trajectory took a sharp ascent with the establishment of **Calendly**, a platform designed to eliminate the often tedious process of scheduling meetings. Awotona, who poured his life savings into the venture, transformed his impatience and unique vision into a pioneering tech solution. With his keen understanding of user experience, Awotona created a product that resonates with millions worldwide, resulting in an impressive valuation for Calendly - the enterprise is reported to be worth around $3 billion.

Throughout his entrepreneurial journey, Awotona displayed a distinctive aptitude for embracing risk. Instead of following a safer path, he saw every challenge as an opportunity, demonstrating resilience and a commitment to his vision that eventually yielded tremendous success.

Calendly's growth under Awotona's stewardship has been remarkable, leading him to be recognised as one of America's wealthiest immigrants. Despite the significant challenges he faced, including navigating the complexities of the tech industry as an immigrant, Awotona's unwavering focus on solving a universal problem propelled him to the ranks of the world's most successful entrepreneurs.

Apart from his contribution to the tech industry through Calendly, Awotona's story is inspiring a new generation of entrepreneurs, particularly from underrepresented backgrounds. His entrepreneurial journey, filled with risks, setbacks, and ultimately, enormous success, serves as a beacon for aspiring tech innovators worldwide.

In recognition of his outstanding contributions, Awotona has achieved billionaire status and continues to steer Calendly towards new heights. His name is synonymous with entrepreneurial resilience, making him a leading figure in the tech industry. Tope Awotona's story is a testament to the potential of a single innovative idea, fuelled by courage, hard work, and determination, to create a global impact.

Tope Awotona, founder of Calendly, is a paragon of entrepreneurial success. He has transformed a personal frustration into a universal solution, leading to the creation of a multi-billion-dollar company. Through his journey, Awotona continues to inspire the next generation of tech entrepreneurs, particularly those from underrepresented backgrounds. His legacy will undoubtedly continue to shape the future of the tech industry.

Ursula Burns, Mechanical Engineer

Next, we have Ursula Burns standing as a beacon in the world of business as the first Black woman to hold the coveted role of CEO in a Fortune 500 company. Her leadership at the forefront of **Xerox Corporation** demonstrated her adept ability to navigate challenging business landscapes, earning her admiration and respect from industry peers and aspiring leaders alike.

As Xerox's CEO from 2009, Burns guided the corporation through turbulent times and swift technological shifts. She pivoted Xerox from its traditional stronghold in printing towards business services, a testament to her foresight and innovative thinking. Simultaneously, she embodied the perfect balance between her career and personal life, serving as an exemplar for those grappling with the challenges of maintaining work-life harmony.

Burns' conviction in her capabilities led her to make bold moves and drive change in the corporate sector. "I'm here because I'm as good as you," she famously stated, affirming her belief in her own abilities and the importance of meritocracy. This focus on her worth and talent, rather than race or gender, has been a powerful testament to her leadership style.

Burns has also been a stalwart advocate for diversity and inclusion, using her influence to mentor and guide countless professionals. Even after leaving Xerox, she has continued to shape the business world through her roles in various corporate boards, including Uber, Exxon Mobil, Nestle, and as Chairwoman of **VEON**, a multinational telecommunications services company.

Burns' remarkable career is peppered with accolades, reflecting her stellar achievements and commitment to fostering a diverse and inclusive corporate culture. Beyond being a trailblazer in business, Burns is a powerful role model, inspiring a new generation of leaders who dare to break barriers and redefine the norms of corporate leadership. Her legacy continues to resonate, demonstrating the vast potential that awaits those willing to follow her.

Rediet Abebe, Computer Scientist

Next, we have Rediet Abebe who stands as an emblem of innovation and perseverance in the world of computer science. With a heart set on using technology as a powerful tool to combat socioeconomic inequality, her journey is nothing short of inspiring. Her groundbreaking contributions as an Ethiopian computer scientist are a testament to her relentless drive to leverage artificial intelligence (AI) in addressing societal issues. Abebe's work has not only influenced her peers but has also ignited the spark of curiosity and ambition in future generations.

In her steady mission to combine AI with economics and social sciences, Abebe has developed remarkable solutions to pervasive societal problems. As a co-founder of the non-profit organisation Mechanism Design for Social Good (MD4SG), she has adeptly applied

<u>computational techniques to enhance societal welfare</u>. This initiative has made tangible changes in communities across the globe, all whilst radiating Abebe's passion for social equity.

At the heart of her philosophy lies the conviction that "AI and algorithms can be designed to promote fairness, to improve social welfare, and to ensure justice." This guiding principle not only fuels her work but also speaks volumes about her commitment to harnessing the potential of technology for the benefit of society. It's through this lens that she approaches her academic contributions, fostering a culture of innovation and critical thinking among the next generation of scientists.

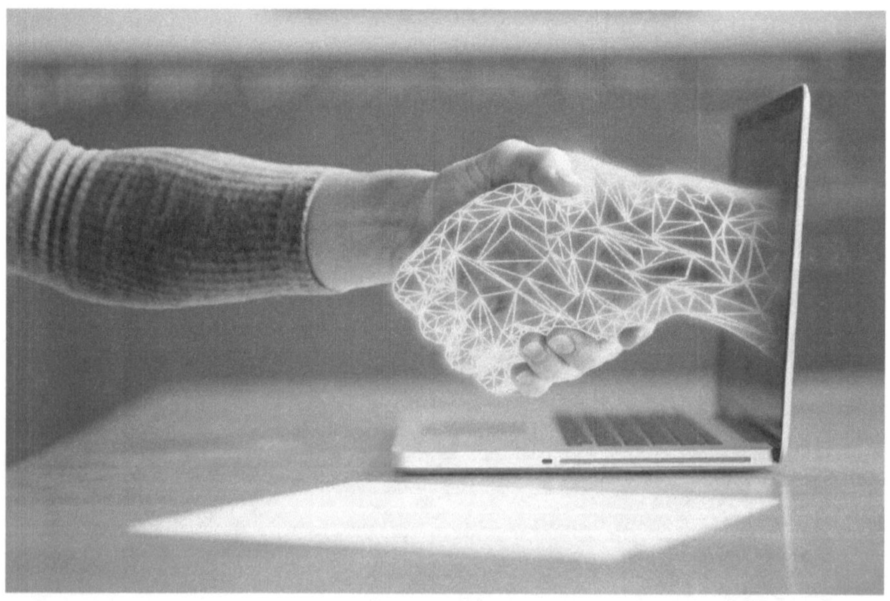

Apart from her monumental work with MD4SG, Abebe's academic contributions have been substantial. As a Junior Fellow at the Harvard Society of Fellows, and the first Black woman to receive a Ph.D. in Computer Science from Cornell University, her influence permeates the academic sphere. She serves as a beacon of diversity and inclusion, inspiring young minds to break through barriers and pursue their passions regardless of their background.

In recognition of her work, Abebe has been presented with many awards. Yet, her greatest achievement lies in her legacy of using AI to promote fairness and justice. As Abebe continues to champion the cause of technological solutions for societal good, she leaves behind an indelible trail of inspiration for all those who dare to dream and disrupt. Rediet Abebe's journey is a testament to the profound impact that one individual can make, encouraging each of us to strive for the betterment of society.

Emeka Afigbo, Electronical Engineer

Last but not least, we have Emeka Afigbo who is an example of innovation and determination in the dynamic arena of technology. His dedication to promoting growth and diversity within the tech industry has distinguished him as a force to be reckoned with. Afigbo's pivotal role in Facebook's developer ecosystem and his current leadership at Okta illuminate his unwavering passion for empowering developers and enhancing technology access.

Afigbo's journey has been defined by his commitment to expand opportunities for developers in Africa. As the head of Developer Programs at Facebook, he amplified Africa's technology representation on the global stage. He was instrumental in launching products like Free Basics and Express Wi-Fi, initiatives designed to provide affordable internet access to underserved areas. Afigbo's work in bridging the digital divide epitomises his passion for social equity and the democratisation of technology access.

At the heart of Afigbo's work is a profound belief that "The next big thing will come out of Africa." This mantra not only fuels his professional endeavours but also underscores his dedication to fostering African innovation in the global tech landscape. His work is a testament to his belief in the untapped potential of African developers, inspiring them to strive for excellence and contribute uniquely to the global tech industry.

Beyond his roles at Facebook and Okta, Afigbo's contributions to the technology community in Africa have been significant. As a mentor and advisor, his influence transcends organisational boundaries. He has been a catalyst in accelerating the growth of numerous startups and tech hubs across Africa, nurturing a vibrant ecosystem of innovation and technological advancement.

Recognition of Afigbo's work extends beyond borders, with numerous accolades honouring his commitment to diversity and empowerment in the tech industry. Yet, his most enduring legacy lies in the thriving community of African developers he has inspired and guided. As Afigbo continues to advocate for diversity and inclusion in technology, he leaves an indelible imprint of inspiration for all aspiring tech enthusiasts. Emeka Afigbo's story is a powerful reminder of the transformative potential of technology, encouraging us all to play our part in shaping a more inclusive and equitable tech future.

Epilogue

The technological landscape we know today would be unrecognisable without the remarkable contributions of the individuals featured in this book. In a deliberate and thoughtful design, the first letter of each name sequentially spells out the title of this work, serving as a subtle yet powerful reminder of the importance of recognising these achievements. However, the innovation and impact of people of colour in the technology sector do not end with the individuals highlighted here.

There are many more pioneers whose contributions merit recognition. This list extends, but is not limited, to names such as Makinde Adeagbo, a software engineer; Leandrew Robinson, CTO of Uncover; Paul Judge, co-founder and CTO of Pindrop; Joy Buolamwini, a renowned computer scientist; Aniyia L. Williams, founder and CEO of Tinsel; Asmau Ahmed, senior strategist; Damilola Odufuwa, Head of Product Communications at Binance Africa; Marlon Nichols, co-founder at MaC Venture Capital; Hemaan Bekele, the inventor of a cancer-fighting soap; Creola Katherine Coleman, mathematician; Hadiyah-Nicole Green, scientist; and Stephanie Alexis Smellie, Head of Creator Partnerships at Spotify, among many others.

As time progresses, more people of colour will undoubtedly shape the future of technology, pushing the boundaries of innovation and redefining industries. It is imperative that these contributions are not overlooked.   The responsibility lies with those who document history to ensure that the remarkable achievements of these individuals are given their rightful place.

This book serves as a testament to the progress made and a call to action for future generations of historians, writers, and industry leaders to continue acknowledging and celebrating the immense value brought to the world by people of colour in technology. The stories told here are but a starting point, and there will undoubtedly be many more works to follow in the years to come.

BIBLIOGRAPHY:

Byron Auguste, "Byron Auguste - President & Co-Founder," Opportunity@Work, https://www.opportunityatwork.org/about-us/team/byron-auguste/..

Auguste, Byron. "Equitable Growth." https://equitablegrowth.org/people/byron-auguste/#:~:text=Auguste%20earned%20a%20B.A.%20summa,Phil/.

Byron Auguste, "Understanding How U.S. Workers Can Benefit from Workplace Automation and Artificial Intelligence," Equitable Growth, https://equitablegrowth.org/understanding-how-u-s-workers-can-benefit-from-workplace-automation-and-artificial-intelligence/.

"Team," Tequitable, https://www.tequitable.com/team.

Ayanna Howard, Sex, Race, and Robots: How to Be Human in the Age of AI, read by Amandla Stenberg, (Grand Haven: Brilliance Audio, 2021), ISBN-13: 9781713621300

Ayanna Howard, "The HistoryMakers," https://www.thehistorymakers.org/biography/ayanna-howard-41.

Johanns, Kate. "Pioneers in Tech: The First African American PhD in Computer Science." Smarter MSP, 12 Feb. 2021, https://smartermsp.com/pioneers-in-tech-the-first-african-american-phd-in-computer-science/.

Clarence G. Williams, The MIT Press; Book and CD-ROM edition (Cambridge, MA: The MIT Press, 2001), 1054, ISBN-13: 978-0262232128.

In Memory of Clarence (Skip) Ellis (1943-2014)," Department of Computer Science, University of Illinois at Urbana-Champaign, https://cs.illinois.edu/news/memory-clarence-skip-ellis-1943-2014.

Kenneth L. Coleman, interviewed by Larry Crowe, The HistoryMakers, April 13, 2007 and June 29, 2022, https://www.thehistorymakers.org/biography/kenneth-l-coleman-41.

"The HistoryMakers: Biography - Kenneth L. Coleman." The HistoryMakers, n.d., https://www.thehistorymakers.org/biography/kenneth-l-coleman-41

Wini Warren, Black Women Scientists in the United States (Bloomington, IN: Indiana University Press, Illustrated edition, 2000), 227-230.

"Bloomberg 50: Odunayo Eweniyi, Damilola Odufuwa - Nigerian Allies." Bloomberg, 3 Dec. 2020, https://www.bloomberg.com/news/articles/2020-12-03/odunayo-eweniyi-damilola-odufuwa-nigerian-allies-endsars-bloomberg-50-2020#xj4y7vzkg.

Valerie Thomas, "Valerie Thomas - Inventor of the Illusion Transmitter," Black Inventor, https://www.black-inventor.com/valerie-thomas.

Odunayo Eweniyi, expert profile, World Bank, https://live.worldbank.org/experts/odunayo-eweniyi.

GeekWire. "Microsoft's next moves: Biz Dev & Strategy leader Christopher Young focusing on key areas." Last modified April 14, 2021. https://www.geekwire.com/2021/microsofts-next-moves-biz-dev-strategy-leader-christopher-young-focusing-key-areas/.

AfroTech, "How Microsoft is Prioritizing Inclusion in Tech," https://afrotech.com/technology-inclusion-microsoft.

YouTube video, "Intro to Computer Science – Chapter 1," posted by freeCodeCamp.org, August 31, 2018, https://www.youtube.com/watch?v=6rqdi2j_Kig.

Full Color Future, "Erica Baker," last modified November 10, 2020, https://fullcolorfuture.org/full-color-50/erica-baker/.

TechCrunch. "Slack's Erica Baker on heads of diversity and the need for inclusion in tech." Interview by Megan Rose Dickey. Last modified February 2, 2016. https://techcrunch.com/2016/02/02/slacks-erica-baker-on-heads-of-diversity-and-the-need-for-inclusion-in-tech/

TechCity NG. "Fireflies AI Co-founder, Sam Udotong's Inspiring Story: From $100, A Failed Pro-Bitcoin Startup to $14m." Last modified August 17, 2018. https://www.techcityng.com/fireflies-ai-co-founder-sam-udotong-s-inspiring-story-from-100-a-failed-pro-bitcoin-startup-to-14m/

Fast Company. "Ime Archibong, Facebook Exec, Discusses What New Tech Companies Can Learn About Diversity From Facebook." Last modified December 2, 2014. https://www.fastcompany.com/3040635/ime-archibong-facebook-exec-discusses-what-new-tech-companies-can-learn-about-diversity-from.

"30 Under 30: Technology Category 2019." Forbes Africa, 1 Jul. 2019, https://www.forbesafrica.com/under-30/2019/07/01/30under30-technology-category-2019/.

"Iyinoluwa Aboyeji." Refined, n.d., https://refinedng.com/iyinoluwa-aboyeji/.

Microsoft, "AI for Accessibility,"
https://www.microsoft.com/en-us/ai/ai-for-accessibility.

InStyle, "This Ex-Google Engineer Who Leaked Salaries Is Advocating for More Inclusion in the Tech World,"
https://www.instyle.com/celebrity/badass-woman-erica-joy-baker

Patch, "CHS' Sam Udotong Awarded National Achievement Scholarship," last modified August 6, 2013, https://patch.com/new-jersey/cinnaminson/chs-sam-udotong-awarded-national-achievement-scholarship.

Nwanji, Ngozi. "Forbes 30 Under 30: Black Honorees." AfroTech, 3 Dec. 2021, https://afrotech.com/forbes-30-under-30-black-honorees.

Ime Archibong, "Ime Archibong," Slush, https://www.slush.org/person/ime-archibong/

Mfonobong Nsehe, "Nnena Ukuku," Forbes, https://www.forbes.com/pictures/fghh45fe/nnena-ukuku-2/?sh=7d30f80c5e04

"Dolby." Dolby Laboratories, n.d., https://www.dolby.com/.

"Dolby Appoints Tony Prophet to its Board of Directors." GlobeNewswire, 8 Dec. 2021, https://www.globenewswire.com/news-release/2021/12/08/2348333/0/en/Dolby-Appoints-Tony-Prophet-to-its-Board-of-Directors.html.

Erich D. Jarvis, "Heads of Laboratories: Erich D. Jarvis," Rockefeller University, https://www.rockefeller.edu/our-scientists/heads-of-laboratories/1159-erich-d-jarvis/.

"Chicago/Turabian Citation Style," Stark State College Library, last modified October 15, 2021, https://libguides.starkstate.edu/c.php?g=1187261&p=8683524.

20th Century Studios, "Hidden Figures – 20th Century Studios | Movies,"

"Ora Lee Smith Home Page," https://oralee.org/.

The Museum of HP Calculators, "HP 95LX Palmtop PC," http://hpmuseum.net/display_item.php?hw=95.

Erika Jefferson, "Where Are the Black Women in STEM Leadership?," Scientific American Blog Network, April 23, 2019, https://blogs.scientificamerican.com/voices/where-are-the-black-women-in-stem-leadership/.

"What Is Dev.to?," Dev.to, https://dev.to/

Annenberg Foundation, "AnnenbergTech,", https://annenberg.org/initiatives/annenbergtech/.

PledgeLA,, https://pledgela.org/.

MTSU News, "NASA Aerospace Engineer Visits MTSU," MTSU News (April 15, 2014), https://mtsunews.com/nasa-aerospace-engineer-visits-mtsu/.

"About PromisePay," PromisePay, https://www.promise-pay.com/about.

"Episode 3: Iheanyi Ekechukwu," People of Color in Tech, https://peopleofcolorintech.com/interview/episode-3-iheanyi-ekechukwu/.

Paul Smith-Goodson, "IBM Research Rolls Out A Comprehensive AI And ML Edge Research Strategy Anchored By Enterprise Partnerships And Use Cases," Forbes, August 8, 2022, https://www.forbes.com/sites/moorinsights/2022/08/08/ibm-research-rolls-out-a-comprehensive-ai-and-ml-edge-research-strategy-anchored-by-enterprise-partnerships-and-use-cases/?sh=613362e713ed

NASA, "STS-8," August 30-September 5, 1983, Space Shuttle program, first night launch and landing, first Foundational Black American astronaut (Guion S. Bluford, Jr.), deployment of Indian National Satellite (INSAT-1B), Space Shuttle Challenger, commanded by Richard H. Truly, piloted by Daniel C. Brandenstein.

"Code2040," https://www.code2040.org/.

EchoVC Partners, "Team," EchoVC Partners, https://www.echovc.com/team.

Footnote: "I'm Here Because I'm as Good as You," *Harvard Business Review*, July 2021, https://hbr.org/2021/07/im-here-because-im-as-good-as-you.

Footnote:"About Us," MD4SG, , https://www.md4sg.com/aboutus.html.

Footnote: "Okta." https://www.okta.com/.

"Nnena Ukuku | Venture Gained Legal PLLC." Venture Gained Legal. https://venturegainedlegal.com/nnena-ukuku.

Techonomy, "Tony Prophet: The Business of Equality," Techonomy, August 11, 2017, https://techonomy.com/conf/te17/detroit-2017/speakers/tony-prophet/.

New Scientist, "Katherine Johnson | Space race mathematician at NASA,"https://www.newscientist.com/people/katherine-johnson/.

D300.org, "D300 Attendance Policy,",
https://www.d300.org/Page/1814.

NPR. (2020, July 10). 'It was personal.' After tragedy, physicist devotes career to cancer research. https://www.npr.org/2020/07/10/888902565/it-was-personal-after-tragedy-physicist-devotes-career-to-cancer-research

Jackson, M. H. and Roy L. Clay. Unstoppable: The Unlikely Rise of Silicon Valley's Babiator Godfather. Amazon, 2021.

Harrero, Sami Haiman. "I Have SOMETHING To Say! Episode #127 – With special guest, Erika Jefferson." YouTube video, April 15, 2022. https://www.youtube.com/watch?v=RClFvKLdr0U.

BWISE. – Black Women in Science and Engineering. http://www.bwiseusa.org/home.html.

Saron Yitbarek, "Saron.io," https://saron.io.

Lydia T. Blanco, "Tech Founder Hadiyah Mujhid Partners with AnnenbergTech and PledgeLA to Create Equity for Black and Latinx VCs and Founders," Forbes, October 9, 2020, https://www.forbes.com/sites/lydiatblanco/2020/10/09/tech-founder-hadiyah-mujhid-partners-with-annenbergtech-and-pledgela-to-create-equity-for-black-and-latinx-vcs-and-founders/?sh=4916d61a2b34.

STEMBoard. https://stemboard.com/.

Bowe, Aisha. "Home." AishaBowe.com. https://www.aishabowe.com/.

Pauleanna Reid, How Phaedra Ellis-Lamkins, CEO Of Promise, Has Leveraged Partnerships To Spare Millions Of Americans From Debt (New York: Forbes,

2021),
https://www.forbes.com/sites/pauleannareid/2021/03
/30/how-phaedra-ellis-lamkins-ceo-of-promise-has-
leveraged-partnerships-to-spare-millions-of-
americans-from-debt/?sh=540a678e3a74.

Nicholas Fuller, PhD, Struggle for Progress,
(Independent Publisher, 2017),
https://www.amazon.com/Struggle-Progress-Nicholas-
Fuller-
PhD/dp/1532329741?#detailBullets_feature_div.

"Iheanyi Ekechukwu," MentorCruise, accessed April
25, 2023,
https://mentorcruise.com/mentor/IheanyiEkechukwu/.

"STS-8," NASA, last modified September 20, 2019,
https://www.nasa.gov/mission_pages/shuttle/shuttle
missions/archives/sts-8.html.

Space Center Houston. "Astronaut Friday: Guion
'Guy' Bluford Jr." Space Center Houston, August 7,
2015, https://spacecenter.org/astronaut-friday-
guion-guy-bluford-jr/

BlackPast. "Bluford, Guion Stewart, Jr. (1942-)."
https://www.blackpast.org/african-american-
history/bluford-guion-stewart-guy-jr-1942/.

Entrepreneur. n.d. "4 Ways Tristan Walker's
Success Depended on Breaking from Tradition."
https://www.entrepreneur.com/starting-a-
business/4-ways-tristan-walkers-success-depended-
on-breaking-from/294245.

Albers, Donald J., and Gerald L. Alexanderson,
eds. 2011. Fascinating Mathematical People:
Interviews and Memoirs. Princeton, NJ: Princeton
University Press. (pp. 193-214).

Blend. "About." https://blend.com/company/about/.

Archetypedi. "About Us."
http://www.archetypedi.com/about-us.

https://calendly.com/en/

"The History Makers," "Ursula Burns," The History Makers,
https://www.thehistorymakers.org/biography/ursula-burns.

Walton, Abriana. "Meet Rediet Abebe, the Ethiopian Computer Scientist Using AI to Fight Socioeconomic Inequality." AfroTech. Access date.
https://afrotech.com/ethiopian-computer-scientist.

Ademiluyi, Tony. "Meet Chukwuemeka Afigbo, Who Bounced Back from Several Canadian Visa Denials to Bestride Google, Facebook and Okta Like a Colossus." Nairametrics, November 6, 2022

InStyle, "This Ex-Google Engineer Who Leaked Salaries Is Advocating for More Inclusion in the Tech World,"
https://www.instyle.com/celebrity/badass-woman-erica-joy-baker

Image Licenses: All Images and Gifs have a free license from Pixabay or was downloaded with a license from Despoitphotos.